A Teacher's Calendar Companion

MAY/JUNE

Creative Ideas to Enrich Monthly Plans!

Written by

Wendy Roh Jenks

Cover Illustration by
Dan Sharp

Inside Illustrations by
Patty McCloskey

Published by Instructional Fair • TS Denison
an imprint of

**McGraw-Hill
Children's Publishing**

About the Author

Wendy Roh Jenks has a bachelor's degree in language arts and elementary education and a master's in reading from Grand Valley State University. Currently in her ninth year of teaching, Wendy teaches third grade in Rockford, Michigan. She has done extensive editing for Instructional Fair • TS Denison. Wendy wrote all ten books in the *A Teacher's Calendar Companion* series.

Credits

Author: Wendy Roh Jenks
Inside Illustrator: Patty McCloskey
Cover Artist: Dan Sharp
Cover Design: Annette Hollister-Papp
Project Director/Editor: Mary Rose Hassinger
Editors: Sara Bierling, Elizabeth Flikkema
Graphic Layout: Tracy L. Wesorick

McGraw-Hill
Children's Publishing
A Division of The McGraw-Hill Companies

Send all inquiries to:
McGraw-Hill Children's Publishing
3195 Wilson Drive NW
Grand Rapids, Michigan 49544

Printed in the United States of America

A Teacher's Calendar Companion: May/June
ISBN: 0-7424-0192-8

1 2 3 4 5 6 7 8 9 05 04 03 02 01

Table of Contents

Morning Routine

Having something prepared for students to do when they first come in the room frees you to do the morning housekeeping tasks, such as reading parent notes, collecting lunch money, and taking attendance. Here is a bouquet of activities to get your May/June days started right.

Activity-a-Day

Use these motivating but simple activities to get your students on track first thing in the morning. Page 5 contains twenty-five activities suitable for K–1 students. Page 6 contains twenty-five activities suitable for students in grades 2–3. Duplicate the appropriate page for your class and use one of the following ideas to manage the selection of activities.

Activity Calendar

Duplicate the appropriate activity sheet one time. Cut into separate activities. Cut twenty-five rectangles (5 cm x 10 cm) out of construction paper. Fold each rectangle in half. Glue one activity inside each folded rectangle. Hang the activities up on a calendar so there is one activity for each school day this month.

Individual Calendars

Duplicate the appropriate activity sheet—one for each student. Students may cut apart the activities and glue them on their own calendars in any order they choose. Each day, students consult their own calendars for their activity choices.

Envelope of Activities

Duplicate the appropriate activity sheet—one for each student. Students cut apart the activities and put them in an envelope. Each day, students choose one activity from their envelopes. Have students glue their activity square to the top of the paper on which they complete the activity.

Activity Journals

Make a journal for each student by stapling lined paper between two construction-paper covers. Students should date the page before completing each activity.

Enlarge and Post the Activity

Use a copy machine to enlarge each activity so it can be posted on a bulletin board. Make a special spot on the board where the students look each morning for the designated activity of the day.

Morning Motivators

Question of the Day

Write a question on the chalkboard each morning for students to answer in their journals. Relate questions to a current social studies, science, or math topic. Questions could be about basic trivia or relating to people all of the students know.

Riddle of the Day

Write a riddle or joke on the chalkboard. Students read and respond.

Language Activity

Write a sentence on the chalkboard with several grammar or spelling mistakes. Students copy the sentence and make all the appropriate corrections.

Finish the Picture

Draw part of a picture or shape on the chalkboard. Have the students copy the drawing and complete the picture.

Activity Board Activities

K–1

Tell a friend ten special things about May. 	Draw a picture of yourself to give to your mother or dad.	Make a flower bookmark. 	Explain to a friend what having a green thumb means.	Draw a maypole with colorful streamers.
Finish this sentence: "On Memorial Day my family…" 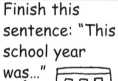	Finish this sentence: "This school year was…" 	Tell a friend about a great summer vacation idea. 	Draw your favorite summer sport. 	Draw and color a flower garden with four types of flowers.
Draw 2 + 3 flowers. Add a bee to one of the flowers. 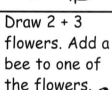	Draw and color a May basket. 	Tell a friend the names of the summer months. June August 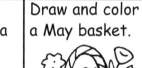	Draw and color an American flag. 	Cut five words from a newspaper that begin with the letter M. mockingbird 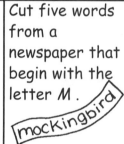
Tell a friend about a special celebration you've attended. 	Tell a friend about your family. 	Tell a friend ten special things about June. 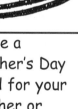	Make a Mother's Day card for your mother or grandmother. I Love MOM	Draw and color a picnic basket with your favorite foods in it.
Cut five words from a magazine that begin with the letter J. 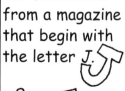	Draw a picture of your favorite school activity. 	Make a Father's Day card for your father or grandfather. Grandpa 	Draw ten flowers. Count by 2s as you point to each flower.	Count by 5s, from 5 to 105. 

5   IF8468 *May/June*

Activity Board Activities

2–3

Write a list of ten special things about May.	Draw a picture of yourself to give your mom or dad. Make a frame.	Plan a scavenger hunt. Make a list of ten things to find.	Design a flower bookmark for a friend.	Write a story about a farmer and his crops.
Draw a maypole with colorful streamers.	Finish this sentence: "On Memorial Day we remember…"	Finish this sentence: "This was a great year because…"	Plan a summer vacation. Draw a map to go with your plan.	Draw a flower garden. Label four types of flowers.
Draw yourself doing an outdoor activity in the spring.	Draw 14 – 7 flowers with 9 – 5 bees on them.	List the summer months. Write three words to describe each. Hot Sunny	Write a poem about your favorite warm weather activity.	Draw a plan for growing a vegetable garden. Color and label rows. carrots beans
Draw and color the American flag. Write three facts about the flag.	List your three favorite books and say why you like each.	Draw and color a piñata for a Cinco de Mayo celebration.	List ten things that are easier to do in June than in December.	Design a Mother's Day card for your mother or grandmother. I LOVE GRANDMA
Write a thank-you note to a person that made this year special. Thank You!	Finish this sentence: "On Flag Day we commemorate…"	Plan a picnic menu. Draw and color a great picnic spot.	Draw a picture of your favorite school activity.	Design a Father's Day card for your father or grandfather. DAD

IF8468 May/June

May/June Calendars

Classroom Calendar

Reinforce calendar concepts and support your math curriculum by having a classroom calendar. Set aside a time each day to discuss skills appropriate to your class's needs. Here are some activities to do during calendar time.

- Identify today, yesterday, and tomorrow.
- Identify the date.
- Keep track of how many school days there have been with a number line and tallies. Teach place value by looking for number patterns.
- Look at patterns created on the calendar by using a combination of shapes and colors for the dates.
- Identify birthdays, holidays, or other special events. Count days remaining until the event. Have students predict what pattern shape will fall on a certain day.
- Record the day's weather.

- Talk about different ways to represent the number of the date. For example, on May 12, students may list 6 + 6, 9 + 3, one dozen, 4 x 3, etc.
- Write on date shapes to keep track of important events for the day. Create a journal of the month's activities by gluing the shapes into a May/June book.

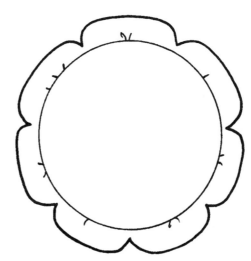

Individual Student Calendars

Duplicate page 8 for each student. Use this calendar in a variety of ways. Choose one or two of the following activities to complement class studies.

- On the first day, write in the dates for the whole month. Add special assignments and events.
- Each day, write the date. Fill in weekend dates on Mondays.
- Each morning, have students name the complete date, yesterday's day and date, and tomorrow's day and date.
- Maintain a design pattern across the calendar days. For example, have students draw a flower on day one, a beach ball on day two, and a flag on day three. Students should repeat the pattern throughout the month and look for diagonal and vertical patterns that develop.

- On each calendar day, students write different ways to represent that number. For example, on June 24, students write 23 + 1, 12 x 2, 50 – 26, two dozen, etc.
- Use the calendar as an incentive chart. Place stickers on student calendars for good behavior or great work.
- Use the calendar as a class incentive chart. At the end of the month, students may be awarded small candies if they have earned a given number of stickers on the class calendar. Stickers may be awarded for good behavior or good work.

Sunday	Monday	Tuesday	Wednesday	Thursday	Friday	Saturday

Parent Connections

Newsletters

Send home a weekly newsletter to regularly communicate with parents what is happening in the classroom. See pages 11 and 12 for reproducible outlines of weekly newsletters. The following are different approaches to communication with parents.

On Monday, send home a newsletter that indicates the major themes, skills, books, and events of the upcoming week. Use the outline on page 11. At the bottom of the page are sentences for the students to complete at home about their week at school. This is a great way for students to reflect on the important events and lessons of the week. Have students return the sentences at the beginning of the following week.

On Friday, send home the newsletter on page 11 with descriptions of lessons, books, and events in the past week. Have students help you write the newsletter. Duplicate the completed newsletter for each student. Have them complete the sentences on the bottom of the page before they take it home.

Send home a newsletter that is based on the skills, themes, and events of each curriculum area you will be studying in the upcoming or past week. Have the students help you write the newsletter or ask students to add illustrations. Use the reproducible outline on page 12.

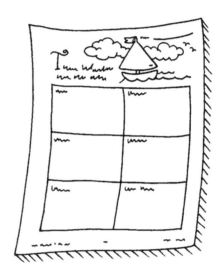

Daily Log

When parents ask, "What did you do today?" they often hear, "I don't know." Help students form their answers in advance by writing a daily log. Students fill out a daily log at the end of each day with a description of the most important events of the day (see page 13 for the May/June Daily Log). Younger students can copy a sentence from the chalkboard or draw a picture. As an alternative, end your day with a brainstorming session about what students learned that day. Write their responses in the outline on page 13. Reproduce the Daily Log to send home on Friday.

Quality-Time Activities

Give parents ideas of quality activities they can do at home with their children. At the beginning of the month, send home the May/June Quality-Time Activities sheet on page 14.

Reading Log

To encourage at-home reading, send home a reading log. Students keep track of the books they have read during the month (see page 15). Older students can read and record their own books while younger students can record books that others have read to them. When students return the logs at the end of the month, they can share their favorite book of the month with the rest of the class. Offer small incentives, such as a bookmark, for each returned reading log. A pizza lunch can be awarded at the end of a semester or the school year for those who returned all of their logs throughout the year or during a specific period of time.

School-to-Home Connections

Sharing Bag

A sharing bag can be a cloth bag, backpack, or even a paper sack that goes home with each student in the class—one at a time. Each time it goes home, the student works with his or her family to add to the bag according to the directions. The student shares his or her work with the rest of the class the next day and passes the bag on to the next student. To add interest, put other items in the bag related to the activity, such as a book, a plush toy, or a treat. One of the wonderful results of the sharing bag is that students and their families look forward to seeing what is in the bag, reading other students' work, and adding to the bag.

For May and June's sharing bag, have your students invent or "discover" a new plant. Place a notebook in the bag with the following letter glued to the inside front cover.

> Dear Parents,
>
> On the next available page in this notebook, help your child draw and then write about a plant that he or she has "discovered" or created. Include in your description how the plant grows, whether it has fruit, flowers, or seeds, and what its uses are. The description should be four to five sentences.
> Please return the notebook and the sharing bag on the next school day. Your child will be sharing his or her discovery with the rest of the class.
> Thank you for your help.
>
> Sincerely,

Younger students may dictate their stories to an adult. Modify the directions to reflect this, if necessary. Set aside time each day for sharing and put the notebook in your reading center when all the students have contributed to the project.

Awards and Incentives

Use awards and incentive charts to give your students positive feedback and to build self-esteem (see pages 16 and 17 for examples). Use the incentive chart individually or as a class to keep track of progress toward a specific goal. Place stickers in the squares as progress is made. Reward students with extra recess time, a no-homework pass, free time, or lunch with the teacher.

The stationery on pages 18 and 19 can be used for letters to parents, students, or other staff members. Use the stationery in the printer to create classroom posters and signs.

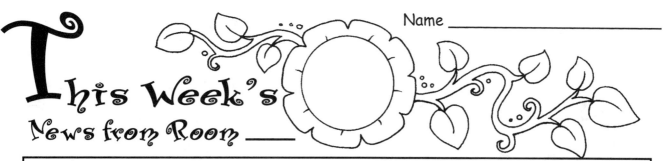

Name _____

This Week's
News from Room ____

Monday	
Tuesday	
Wednesday	
Thursday	
Friday	

For Your Information _____

_____

Looking Back at My Week

The most important thing I learned this week was _____

_____.

The thing I need to continue to work on the most is _____

_____.

I did something nice for someone when I _____

_____.

One word to describe my week is _____.

Name _____

This Week's
News from Room ___

Math	Reading
Science	**Writing**
Spelling	**Social Studies**

         IF8468 *May/June*

Name _____

Daily Log

Week of _____

Monday

Tuesday

Wednesday

Thursday

Friday

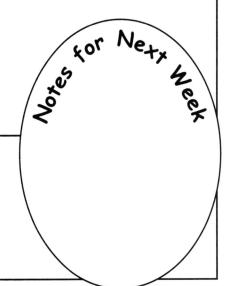

Notes for Next Week

May/June Quality-Time Activities

Share these activities with your child during May and June.

1. Have your child draw May and June calendars. Mark off each day together.

2. Have your child say as many one-syllable words as he or she can in two minutes.

3. Have your child name words that begin with each letter in the word *maypole*.

4. Help your child set three goals to reach before the end of the school year.

5. Have your child write a thank-you note to someone who helped make school special.

6. Have your child find the history of the Mexican celebration of Cinco de Mayo.

7. Have your child finish this statement: "Our best summer vacation was when..."

8. Help your child look up five countries and write two sentences about each.

9. Take a nature walk. Collect and press a variety of leaves.

10. Have your child find out what red, white, and blue symbolize in the American flag.

11. Give your child one outdoor responsibility and encourage follow-through by using a checklist or incentive chart.

12. Have your child choose one outdoor plant and help keep a record of its growth and change.

13. Have your child name five things learned in each subject this school year.

14. Have your child plan a Mexican fiesta that includes a food such as tacos.

15. Plan a family scavenger hunt. Help your child write a list for each family member.

16. Have your child find and write three facts about Memorial Day.

17. Have your child interview family members and write a family history book.

18. Make a potato stencil. Cut a potato in half and carve the design inside. Help dip in paint or food coloring and press on paper.

19. Make finger paint for outdoor fun. Mix liquid starch with colored tempera paint. Spread on wet paper.

20. Have your child make a greeting card for a special older person.

21. Help your child start a summer nature collection.

22. Have a picnic with your child. Help him or her plan the menu.

23. Go to the library and check out books on Betsy Ross and the American flag.

24. Have your child give you oral directions for how to play a favorite sport.

25. Help your child plan an Olympic event, complete with games, paper medals, and balloons.

26. Visit a greenhouse together and count how many different types of flowers you see.

27. Have your child write a rhyming poem about the summer season.

28. Have your child tell why he or she likes to spend time with a certain family member.

29. Have your child help plan a family outing or vacation. Start a list of things to do and bring.

30. Help create a thank-you note for someone in the military service.

Name _____

May / June Reading Log

	Title	Author	Comments
1.			
2.			
3.			
4.			
5.			
6.			
7.			
8.			
9.			
10.			

Something Sweet
to Buzz About!

Name _____

Date _____

For _____

Your Work
Is in Full Bloom!

Name _____

Date _____

For _____

IF8468 May/June

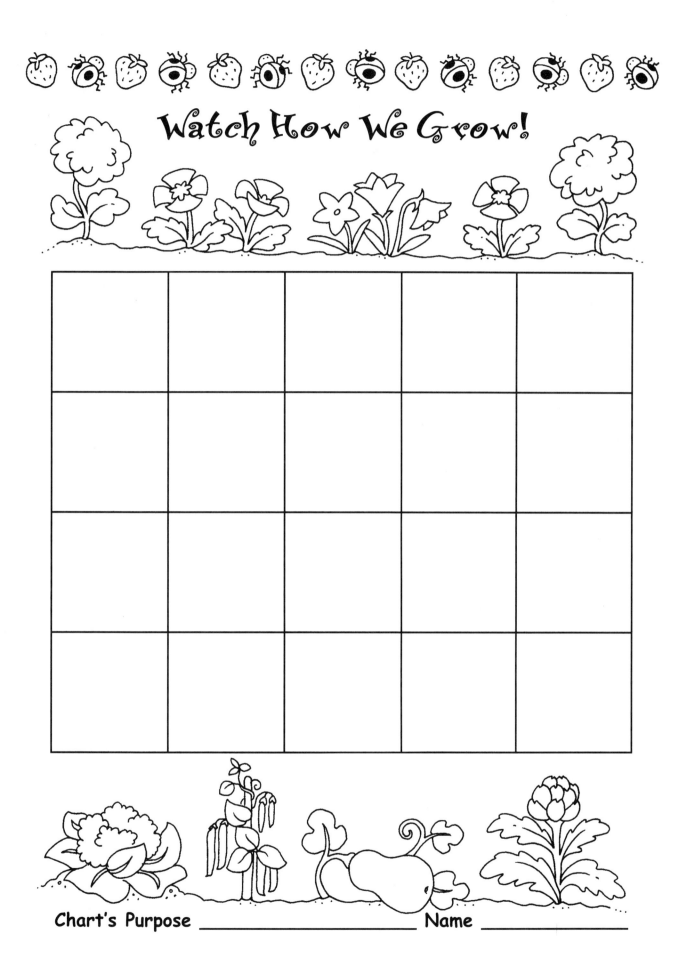

Watch How We Grow!

Chart's Purpose _____   Name _____

17   IF8468 *May/June*

18

IF8468 May/June

IF8468 May/June

Bulletin-Board Brainstorms

A Garden of Learning

Showcase your students' best work on this bulletin board.

1. Have your students make construction paper flowers. Glue their photos in the center of the flowers. This may be an extra copy of a school picture or a snapshot.

2. Add dimension and details to the flowers using tissue paper, glitter, sequins, or other art materials.

3. Have your bulletin board ready with the title **A Garden of Learning**.

4. Attach the flowers to appropriately-sized stems and add to the bulletin board. Attach at least one leaf to each stem.

5. Each week, have your students choose one of their assignments that they think are the best or most interesting and hang the papers from the leaves.

Shades of Summer

Students can share their summer plans using this bulletin board display.

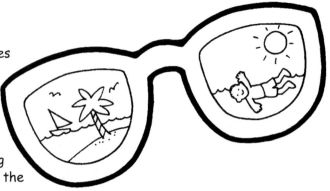

1. Supply each student with a 12" x 18" (30 cm x 46 cm) sheet of construction paper. Students fold the paper horizontally and draw half a pair of sunglasses on the fold (only the frame). Make the frame a double line so that the glasses can be cut out.

2. Leaving the paper folded, cut the glasses out so that, when unfolded, there is a complete pair of sunglasses.

3. Glue the sunglass frames onto white construction paper.

4. Students draw and color scenes showing their summer plans inside the lenses of the frames.

5. Cut out the sunglasses and display on a bulletin board titled **Shades of Summer**.

Literature Focus

May is a great time to read books with a gardening theme.

Cooney, Barbara. *Miss Rumphius*. New York: Viking Press, 1982.

This story is about Alice Rumphius, a woman who fulfilled a promise she made to her grandfather to do something to make the world more beautiful.

Heller, Ruth. *The Reason for a Flower*. New York: Price Stern Sloan Publishing, 1983.

This is a nonfiction book about flowers. The information is presented in rhyme, and is complemented by beautiful illustrations.

Lobel, Anita. *Alison's Zinnia*. New York: Greenwillow Books, 1990.

This book features a flower for every letter of the alphabet.

Stewart, Sarah. *The Gardener*. New York: HarperCollins, 1997.

This book contains a series of letters relating what happens when Lydia Grace goes to live in the city with her Uncle Jim after her father loses his job. Her love of gardening serves as a comfort to her during the difficult time.

Van Allsburg, Chris. *The Garden of Abdul Gasazi*. Boston: Houghton Mifflin Company, 1979.

This story is about a boy named Alan who is caring for a dog that runs away into the forbidden garden of a retired magician.

Read the following book on May 1, celebrated as May Day in some places.

Mora, Pat. *The Rainbow Tulip*. New York: Viking Children's Books, 1999.

A Mexican-American girl experiences the difficulties and joy of being different when she wears a tulip costume for the school May Day parade.

Read books that have information about Cinco de Mayo.

Menard, Valerie. *The Latino Holiday Book: From Cinco de Mayo to Dia de Los Muertos: The Celebrations and Traditions of Hispanic-Americans*. New York: Marlowe and Company, 2000.

Palacios, Argentina. *Viva Mexico! The Story of Benito Juarez and Cinco de Mayo*. Austin: Raintree/Steck-Vaughn, 1996.

Vazquez, Sarah. *A World of Holidays—Cinco de Mayo*. Austin: Raintree/Steck-Vaughn, 1999.

More Book Picks/Silent Reading Club

Here are some books about special mothers and fathers.

Bunting, Eve. *A Perfect Father's Day*. New York: Clarion Books, 1993.

A four-year-old girl plans the perfect day, full of her father's favorite activities.

Joffe Numeroff, Laura. *What Mommies Do Best/What Daddies Do Best*. New York: Simon & Schuster, 1998.

Two stories in one are presented in this book. One features a mother as the main character, and the other a father.

Neitzel, Shirley. *We're Making Breakfast for Mother*. New York: Greenwillow Books, 1997.

Rhymes and rebuses show children making breakfast for their mother; told in a pattern similar to the classic "This is the house that Jack built…"

Smalls-Hector, Irene. *Kevin and His Dad*. Boston: Little, Brown, and Company, 1999.

Kevin spends an entire wonderful day working and playing with his father.

Zolotow, Charlotte. *This Quiet Lady*. New York: Greenwillow Books, 1992.

A child finds out about her mother's early life by looking at old pictures.

Here is a special selection focusing on Flag Day.

Mandrell, Louise. *A Mission for Jenny: A Story about the Meaning of Flag Day*. New York: Summit Publishing Group/Legacy Press, 1993.

Silent Reading Club

Set aside time each day for silent reading. Provide an incentive, such as having several books in the room following a basic theme or genre, and offer a small reward after reading a certain number of books in that group. Invite students to share a favorite book to stimulate interest in it from the other students.

Post favorite books on a May or June bulletin board called, "Fishing for a Great Book." Have students write the titles and authors of their favorite books on fish cutouts (see page 31 for pattern) and add them to a blue construction-paper pond. Add fishing poles and paper cattails. Use this as a way of keeping track of how many books students read during the months of May and June. Students may use the bulletin board as a resource for choosing books to read.

Choral Readings

A great way to get students interested in poetry and help reading fluency is by doing choral readings. Choral reading is when students read a selection aloud. At first, the readings should be done as a class. When the students are more familiar with the piece, the teacher can assign parts to smaller groups or the individuals. Here are suggested methods for choral reading.

- Put a copy of a poem on an overhead for students to read.

- Give a "poem of the week" to the students on Monday and use it for choral readings throughout the week. On Friday, give students a chance to read the poem alone or in a small group. They may be creative with their presentation by acting it out in some way or by using small props.

- Give copies of several poems to students at the beginning of the month. The leader of the day chooses the one to be read that day.

- Incorporate poetry that has a theme to go along with other content areas such as math or science.

Here are some great resources for May and June poetry.

Kennedy, X.J. and Dorothy M. Kennedy, comp. *Talking Like the Rain: A Read-To-Me Book of Poems*. Boston: Little, Brown & Co., 1992.

This is a collection of poetry with many themes, including several poems about families.

Lansky, Bruce, comp. *No More Homework! No More Tests!: Kids' Favorite Funny School Poems*. New York: Meadowbrook Press, 1997.

Celebrate the end of the school year with poems about school.

Withers, Carl, comp. *A Rocket in My Pocket: The Rhymes and Chants of Young Americans*. New York: Henry Holt, 1998.

This classic includes humorous rhymes, counting and jump rope rhymes, songs, chants and tongue twisters.

Reading Buddies

Cross-age tutoring and reading are beneficial for both the older and younger students involved. Establish a reading partnership with a class that is an age that works well with your students. It is helpful for students to keep the same buddy for a least a month in order to build a rapport with each other. Older students may read to the younger ones, and the younger students listen or read their daily assignments. Students share books they have written and practiced, or work together on a selected activity. The following is a suggestion for a May or June activity.

Flip Books

Have your reading buddies pair up to make silly flip books.

1. Provide each pair with an empty flip book. Make this by folding three sheets of 8 1/2" x 11" (22 cm x 28 cm) paper in half lengthwise. Staple across the top of the folded edge. Cut two evenly-spaced slits from the bottom up to make three sections (don't go all the way to the top). On the top page of each section, write the words, **Who? What?** and **Where?**.

2. As a group, brainstorm lists of answers to the questions **Who? What?** and **Where?**

List them on the chalkboard or on chart paper. For example, **Who?**—The girl, **What?**—jumped rope, **Where?**—at school.

3. Have the buddies choose five answers from each list to write in the sections of their book. Illustrate the phrases.

4. By randomly flipping the pages, students will read silly sentences. Have reading partners trade with other pairs of buddies and share their books.

1.

Who what where

2.

who	what	where
the girl	jumped rope	on the playground
the boy	rode a bike	to the park
the cat	took a nap	in a chair

3.

The girl | jumped rope | on the playground

4.

A Puppet Play

Here is a story that can be performed as a puppet play or as a readers' theater. To do as a puppet play, first have your students make the puppets by duplicating pages 26 and 27 for each student. Have students color, cut, and glue each puppet to a craft stick. Assign reading parts to small groups of seven, with two narrators and five students to work the puppets while they say their lines. As a follow up activity, students may write their own puppet shows using the same puppet characters. Performances may be for the rest of the class or for your reading partner group.

A Late Bloomer

Parts:	Narrator 1	Daisy	Tulip	Petunia
	Narrator 2	Girl	Mother	

Narrator 1: Once upon a time, there were three flowers living on a table in a greenhouse. It was early spring and they were waiting to be sold.

Narrator 2: One flower was a sunny daisy, one was a colorful tulip, and one was a petunia. The petunia had not yet bloomed and did not show any color. Days went by and no one stopped to look at the petunia.

Narrator 1: One day, the three flowers were talking.

Daisy: "Tulip! Isn't it great to be open and see the light?"

Tulip: "Oh yes! It will only be a matter of time before someone buys us and plants us in the ground. It will feel great to stretch out our roots."

Daisy: "I agree. Petunia, when do you think you'll be sold?"

Petunia: "I don't know."

Narrator 2: Petunia was feeling very sad. She thought no one would ever look at her before her flower bloomed and she didn't think that would ever happen.

Tulip: "Who's going to buy Petunia? People want flowers with color, like us."

Daisy: "You're right, Tulip. Who would want her?"

Narrator 1: Petunia wilted just a little with sadness. Soon, a little girl and her mother came walking down the aisle in the greenhouse. They were looking for flowers to plant in their yard.

Narrator 2: The mother gently picked up Petunia and said to her daughter,

Mother: "What do you think about this one?"

 IF8468 May/June

Girl: "It isn't very pretty. And there's no flower, Mommy!"

Mother: "There will be. See this part here?"

Narrator 1: The mother gently touched the bud of Petunia's flower, and explained how the flower would bloom in time.

Girl: "Okay, let's get that one. It will be fun to watch it bloom."

Petunia: "I can't believe it! I'm so happy to be chosen! Goodbye, Tulip! Goodbye, Daisy!"

Tulip: "What? That girl is picking Petunia? I can't believe it."

Daisy: "Be careful, Petunia. She'll probably break your stem while she's planting you."

Narrator 2: But Petunia was so happy she didn't mind what Tulip and Daisy had to say. When the girl and her mother got home, they planted Petunia in a warm and sunny spot in their yard.

Narrator 1: The sun and soil felt so good to Petunia. Three days later, while the girl was outside playing, she noticed that Petunia had bloomed. She was the most beautiful bright pink flower she had ever seen.

Girl: "Petunia, my mother was right! You are so pretty!"

Petunia: "If only Tulip and Daisy could see me now!"

All: The end.

Puppet Patterns

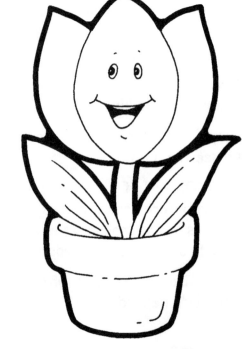

Puppet Patterns

IF8468 *May/June*

Writing Activities

Another Story About a Late Bloomer

Get your students thinking about something they have accomplished this school year that required hard work to achieve. Read the following book to your class:

Kraus, Robert. *Leo the Late Bloomer*. New York: Windmill Books, 1971.

This is a story about a young tiger who does not learn at the same rate as other animals. His father worries until, one day, Leo finally blooms.

Brainstorm and then discuss things the class had to work hard at to learn. Were there times when they felt they would never "bloom?" Have them think of a time and write about it on a duplicate of page 29. Put the pages together in a class book.

A Bouquet of Writing Activities

Display great writing activities for May and June.

1. Cut eight flowers from an assortment of colored paper.

2. Write one of the following activities on each of the flowers.

Write as many words as you can using the letters in the words *spring flowers*.

Design a new flower. Name it. Write a paragraph describing the flower.

Write a poem about flowers.

Write five facts about flowers.

Finish this story, "When the red tulip began to open..."

Finish this story, "As the girl picked the big yellow sunflower…"

Finish this story, "As the boy quickly walked through the flower garden…"

Finish this story, "The dog thought it heard something in the flower bed…"

3. Paste each flower on a craft stick that is painted green.

4. Fill a clay pot with dirt.

5. Cut an extra flower. Write "Please, pick the flowers!" on it and tape or glue the flower to the pot.

6. Place the flowers in the pot and put in a writing center.

My "Blooming" Story

Finish the statements on the flower below.
Write about something you do better now than you did at the beginning of the school year.
Explain what you did to become better, and how you feel about it now.

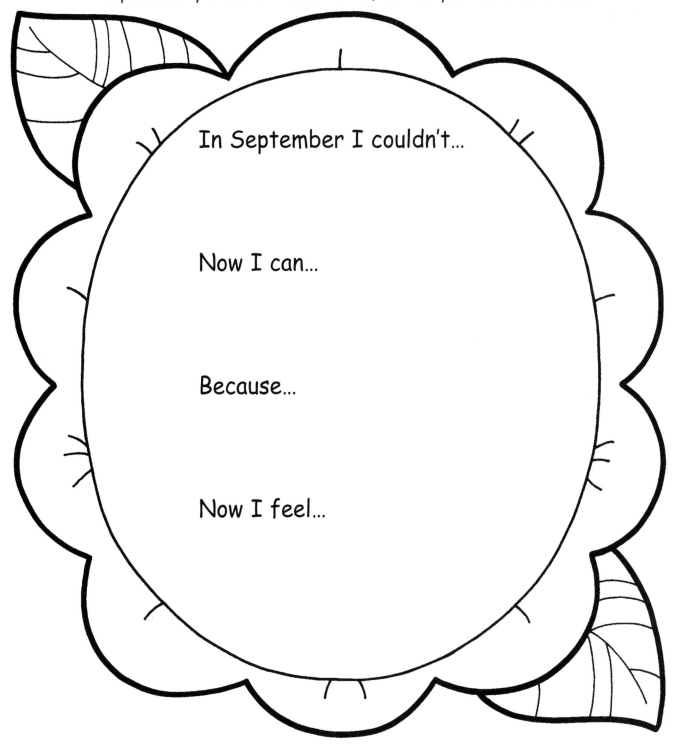

In September I couldn't...

Now I can...

Because...

Now I feel...

29   IF8468 *May/June*

Make the Most out of This

Here is a creative writing activity that will get your students' imaginations flowing. Read the following book to your students.

Barrett, Judi. *Things That Are Most in the World*. New York: Atheneum, 1998.

Each page in this book describes something that is "most" in the world. It follows the pattern, "The _____ est thing in the world is _____," and provides a blank page at the back of the book to duplicate for students' writing.

Give your students a duplicate of the last page of the book and have them come up with their own "most" sentences. Have students make pop-up pages with their ideas.

1. Fold an 8 1/2" x 11" (21 cm x 28 cm) paper in half, across the width of the paper.

2. Cut two slits near the middle on the folded edge of the paper.

3. Fold the paper in the opposite direction. Pop out the segment made from the cut and fold to make a right-angle box inside the folded paper.

4. Fold a second piece of paper and glue the first cut paper inside.

5. Draw and color a picture of what the "most" sentence is about, cut it out, and glue it on the section that pops out.

6. Draw a background to go with the part that pops out.

7. Copy the sentence from the edited paper so that the first part is on the cover of the folded sheet and the last part is on the inside, under the pop-out illustration.

8. Display them in a hallway for others to predict and enjoy.

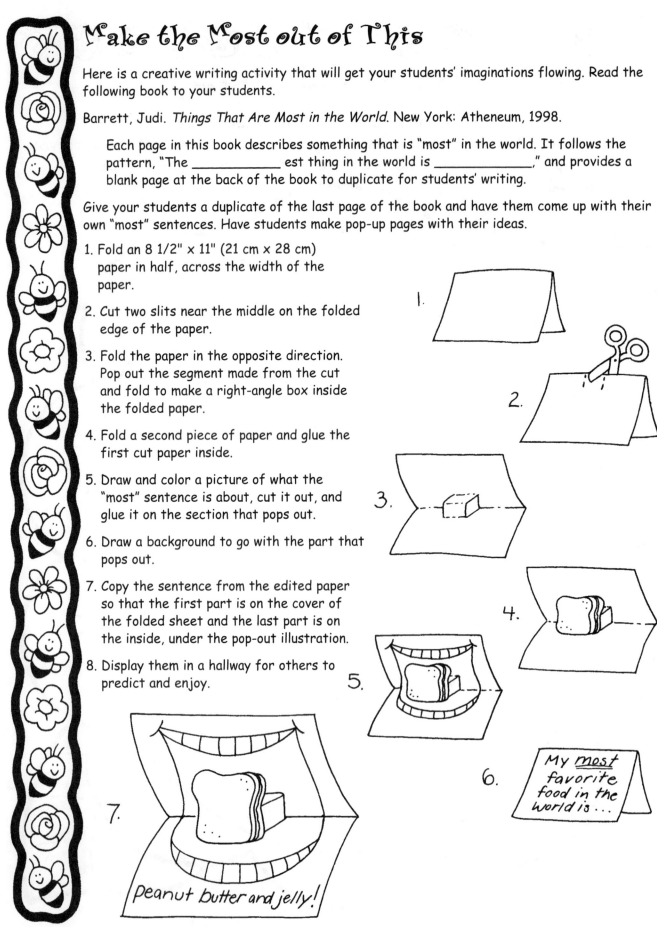

6. My *most* favorite food in the world is...

7. Peanut butter and jelly!

Math Focus

Everything's Coming up Numbers

Help students practice showing different names for numbers or equivalent math problems.

1. Make several tag board cutouts of a flower shape (see pattern below).

2. Make four times as many petal cutouts as flowers. The petals should be the same size as the petals on the flower shapes.

3. Write math problems that all equal the same number on four of the petals. In the center of a flower, write the answer to the problems. Students lay the four petals on the flower shape to match the problems with the answer. Make a set of four petals for each flower.

4. Write the problems appropriate to your students needs. Younger students could match tally marks, number words, or pictures equaling the number in the center of the flower.

5. Place in a math center.

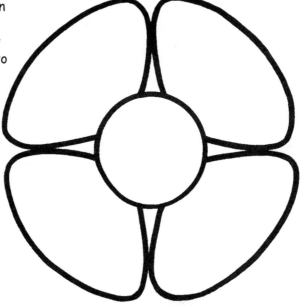

Fish Concentration

Practice a variety of skills using this fish concentration game. Cut an even number of fish so that you can write problems on half the fish and answers on the other half. Tailor the game to fit your students' needs. Some possibilities are basic addition, subtraction, or multiplication facts, coin combinations that equal the same amount, analog and digital clocks that say the same time, patterns of numbers in which one fish is a continuation of another, or pictures showing equivalent numbers. Students play by taking turns flipping fish over until they match a problem with an answer. The player with the most matches when all the fish are gone wins.

Estimation and Graphing

Estimation Jar

Here are some great May and June fillers for an estimation jar in your room: seeds, red, green, and white candies, flag and flower stickers, marbles, and pencils. At the end of the first week, sort several of the students' estimations into "too high" and "too low" categories. This will guide estimations for the following weeks. Count the items by tens and ones. Determine which estimates are the closest. If the item in the jar is something the students may keep, determine as a class how to divide the items equally.

Seed Sort

This graphing activity can be done as a whole class or placed in a math center. Give each child a small cup or bag of assorted seeds. Provide a blank graph like the one in the illustration below. Have the students sort their seeds by type. Count how many they have of each kind. Then have the students fill in the graph by writing or drawing in the kinds of seeds, and then coloring each section to show the number of each seed they counted. Discuss the data on the graphs with questions such as, "How many more brown seeds than white seeds?"

Student Favorites

Take some time to graph student favorites. Here are some examples:

- favorite book the teacher read aloud this year
- favorite class book they wrote
- favorite science project or lesson of the year
- favorite math activity
- favorite art project
- favorite subject
- favorite reading partner activity

Narrow down the list to four or five choices for each category to make graphing manageable. Brainstorm class favorites and then vote to determine the top four or five. Provide a graph with the choices listed and have your students poll each other to complete their graphs.

Science Focus—Climbing Water

This experiment will show students how plants get water from the soil. The tendency for water to climb into the very small spaces that are present in porous materials is called capillary action. This experiment will reinforce the following concepts:

- Water molecules are attracted to each other.

- Liquids are attracted to other substances.

- Liquids will move upward through small openings against the force of gravity.

The Experiment

Materials Needed:

paper towels	food coloring
tissues	water
napkins	plastic cups

This activity should be done with the entire class. Pass out the worksheet (page 34) and review the instructions together. Demonstrate how to tightly roll the paper towels, tissues, and napkins. Pass out a cup of water with food coloring in it to each student. It is particularly important to encourage students to predict what they think will happen and to record these ideas before completing each part of the exercise. You may also wish to discuss possible outcomes with the class, as a whole.

When everyone is ready, instruct the students to place one end of each paper roll in the cup of water. Students will observe the water climbing up the different paper rolls. The narrower the capillary tubes, the faster the water will climb. The tissue will be soaked first since the weave of that paper is tighter and the tubes are narrower. Have students record the results and propose why they

think the tissue was soaked first.

For the second part of the experiment, students should gently bend the tops of the wet rolls of paper over an empty cup, leaving the bottoms of the rolls still in the water. The water should continue to climb the paper rolls until either the first cup is empty or the water is at equal levels in both cups.

Discuss student findings at the end of your investigation. Encourage your students to verbalize their conclusions and reinforce the main concepts. Have your students think of other real-life applications of the principle of capillary action, such as mops and sponges.

Climbing Water Worksheet

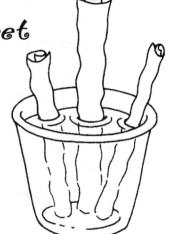

1. Roll a paper towel, a tissue, and a napkin. Predict what might happen if you stand the three rolls of paper in the water to which food coloring has been added.

_____

_____

_____

2. Put the rolls in the water. What happens?

_____

_____

_____

3. Which roll of paper did the water climb up the fastest?

_____

Try This.

4. What do you think will happen if you tip the tops of the wet rolls into an empty cup?

_____

_____

_____

5. Try it. Describe what happened.

_____

_____

6. What do you think would happen if you left the paper overnight?

_____

_____

_____

Art Activity—A May Basket

Each student needs the following:

    a copy of page 36.

    an empty, rinsed half-pint milk carton.

    a piece of colored tissue paper.

    two pipe cleaners, cut in half.

    scissors, glue, and crayons.

1. Cut off the top of the milk carton.

2. Color basket cover from page 36, cut out, wrap, and glue to the carton.

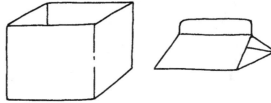

3. Color and cut out four flowers. Fold each in half and paste over the end of a pipe cleaner.

4. Crumple tissue into the basket and place flowers in the basket.

5. Color, cut, bend, and tape a construction paper handle to the sides of the basket.

May Basket Patterns

36

IF8468 May/June

Making May Marvelous

Memorial Day Mobile

1. Provide each student with a pattern of the American flag. This pattern can be 8 1/2" x 11" or larger. Glue onto tag board and color.

2. On yellow stars, have the students copy the following Memorial Day facts.

🍓 **Memorial Day is a US federal holiday.**

🍓 **We honor soldiers on Memorial Day.**

🍓 **There are often parades to celebrate Memorial Day.**

🍓 **The traditional Memorial Day is May 30.**

3. Punch the appropriate number of holes along the bottom of the flag and one in each star.

4. Hang stars from the flag using varying lengths of string or yarn.

5. Hang in the classroom to celebrate Memorial Day.

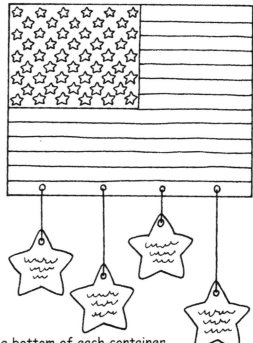

Hanging Flower Basket

Here's a great Mother's Day gift idea.

1. Collect a margarine tub for each student.

2. Have students make a small drainage hole in the bottom of each container.

3. Students fill each container with potting soil and a small annual plant, such as a pansy.

4. Next, students punch three holes in the rim of the tub and tie yarn for hanging the basket.

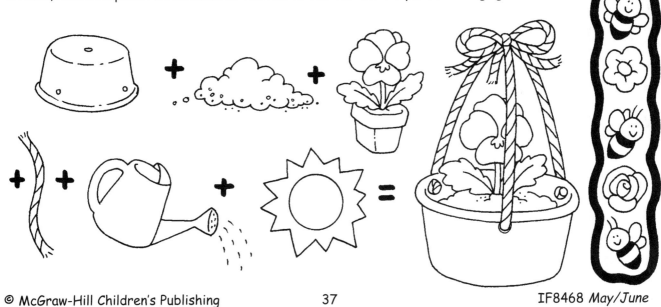

         IF8468 *May/June*

Stained-Glass Butterflies

Materials Needed:

12" x 18" (30 cm x 46 cm) black construction paper (one sheet per student)

assorted colors of tissue paper

scissors

glue

string

Student Directions:

1. Fold the black paper in half.

2. Draw half an outline of a butterfly. (Younger students repeat the outline one inch inside the first outline, as shown. Older students can create more intricate designs.)

or

3. Cut out the insides of the designs, leaving borders as shown.

4. With the design still folded in half, trace the outside shape onto a piece of folded tissue paper and cut out the tissue slightly smaller than the construction paper design. Older students may use different colored tissue for each section.

5. Place the black outline frame over the tissue paper and glue together. Hang the butterfly from the ceiling or place in a window.

Variation:

If hanging the art from the ceiling, two butterfly designs can be cut from construction paper. Glue the tissue between the two pieces for a different effect.

Practice Takes Shape

Copy this page and use as an activity or assignment page. Write activities on sections of the basket and flowers. Fold these directions under and duplicate a page for each student. Make a new copy for each activity.

Suggested activities to write on the flowers and basket:

math problems

blanks for words made from the letters in the words *May Basket*

words appropriate for a May or June creative writing story

color code for students to color by numbers

spelling words for study and definitions

creative story starters

39   IF8468 *May/June*

Special Days

Cinco de Mayo—May 5

This is an important patriotic festival for Mexicans and Mexican-Americans. It helps us remember an important battle in 1861, in which the Mexican Army successfully opposed a French invasion. This holiday celebrates their victory as well as the determination, courage, and independence of Mexico.

Remember Cinco de Mayo with a simple classroom celebration, or fiesta. Decorate the room with green, white, and red streamers. Serve a Mexican dish, such as tacos or enchiladas. Make and break a piñata. Use the directions found on page 41 for making a piñata.

Mother's and Father's Days Letters

Have students write a letter to their mother or father using the templates on page 42. Students should color the border and write six sentences about their parent(s). Sentences should begin with each letter in the words *Mother* and *Father*. Mount the completed letter on a sheet of construction paper.

Love Coupons

Duplicate page 43 for each student. Have students color a cover and the coupons. Cut the coupons out, stack them, punch holes, and tie the pages together with yarn. Have students give the coupon books to their moms, dads, or other special family members.

Flag Day—June 14

Flag Day commemorates June 14, 1777, the day the United States flag was adopted by the Continental Congress. Have your students complete the activity on page 44 to learn more about the flag and the woman who legend says made it—Betsy Ross.

Making a Piñata

Make a simple papier-mâché piñata.

1. Blow up a balloon to the desired size.

2. Mix papier-mâché paste. In a large bowl, slowly mix 1/2 cup (119 ml) flour with 1/4 cup (.12 L) water, stirring so that the flour will not lump. When well blended, add enough water to make a thin paste. Add one tablespoon of white glue or wood glue to the mixture and stir until well-blended. Pour the paste into a wide, shallow pan.

3. Tear or cut newspaper strips, about 1/2 inch (1.3 cm) wide.

4. Dip strips of newspaper in the paste, wiping off any excess. Cover the balloon with the paste-soaked strips of paper, crisscrossing them over the surface to a final thickness of about 1/4 inch (approximately 3–5 layers). Let the balloon dry until it is stiff and holds its shape.

5. When the papier-mâché has dried, lightly go over the surface with sandpaper and then dust with a tissue.

6. Cut a hole through the papier maché and into the balloon. Remove the balloon, if possible.

7. Cover the outside of the piñata with two coats of an acrylic polymer gloss medium. Let dry completely.

8. Paint using acrylic or tempera paints.

9. Put small wrapped candies and gifts into the piñata through the opening you cut. Reattach the cover of the hole to the piñata if you would like.

10. Add a hanging cord to the top of the piñata and decorate with wrapping paper and ruffled tissue paper or construction paper.

11. Hang the piñata at shoulder height or higher.

12. Use a broom handle and have blindfolded participants try to break the piñata by hitting it. The piñata should be raised or lowered at each swing to make it more difficult to hit.

Mother's Day Letter

Dear Mom,

♡ M _____

♡ O _____

♡ T _____

♡ H _____

♡ E _____

♡ R _____

Love, _____

Father's Day Letter

Dear Dad,

☆ F _____

☆ A _____

☆ T _____

☆ H _____

☆ E _____

☆ R _____

SUPER DAD

Love, _____

Love Coupons

Get a Great Big Hug

Set the Table

Get a Special Favor

Your Special Helper

I'll Tell You a Story

Clean Up

Run an Errand

Yard Work

Pick Up

I Love You This Much

IF8468 *May/June*

You're a Grand Old Flag

Learn more about the United States flag and Betsy Ross. Cut off the bottom of this page, cut the facts apart, and glue them on the flag in the correct order.

- cut here -

Betsy Ross made a flag with thirteen stars.

Betsy Ross was born in Philadelphia in 1752.

The new flag was adopted by Congress on June 14, 1777.

Today, we celebrate Flag Day every fourteenth of June.

According to legend, George Washington asked her to make a flag in June, 1776.

As a young woman, she became an expert flag maker.

Just for Fun

A Game Board for May and June:

Make the game board by duplicating the pattern on page 46. Color with markers and glue on a larger piece of poster board. You may want to enlarge, using an opaque projector or overhead, to accommodate more than two players.

To Play:

1. Make sets of game cards out of tag board. Number the cards 1, 2, or 3 on one side and write a question on the other. Game questions could be math problems, questions about a science topic, or questions about a story the entire class has read.

2. Students place their game markers on **Start**. Ideas for game markers include plastic bugs, erasers, and bingo chips. Players take turns picking a question card. If the question is answered correctly, the player moves the number of spaces that is the same as the number listed on the question card.

3. If the question is answered incorrectly, the player does not move.

4. The first player to reach **Finish** wins the game.

Memory Books

See pages 47–48 for a year-end memory-book activity that can be placed in a center, used when students are finished with other work, or used as a whole-class activity. Have students color and complete each section, except for the autograph page. Cut the pages apart, place them in order, punch holes, and tie together with yarn or ribbon. Allow students time to collect autographs from classmates.

IF8468 *May/June*

Start!

Hive Hunt

Bee-utiful weather! Move ahead 1 space.

Oops! Stopped at flower for pollen! Move back 2 spaces!

Oops! Time out for a honey picnic! Lose a turn!

Finish!
Hive
Sweet
Hive

IF8468 May/June

Draw your school here.

My school is _____

My grade is _____

My teacher is _____

My Memory Book

Belongs to: _____

Age: _____

IF8468 *May/June*

Autographs

My Favorites

My favorite month of school is _____

because _____

My favorite holiday is _____

My favorite subject is _____

My favorite book is _____

My favorite part of the day is _____

IF8468 *May/June*